Peaceful Election in Kenya

"...And if we have been blessed by God with this nation, it behoves us as individuals who stake claim to this nation as their home to ensure we protect it, to ensure we safeguard it, to ensure that we live with each other in peace." President Uhuru Kenyatta.

Compiler

ERIC KYALO

A Destiny Ink Production

Noel Lorenz Publications

Asia. Africa. Europe

Title of Book: **Peaceful Election in Kenya**
Author of Book: **ERIC KYALO**
First Published in India in September 2022 by Noel Lorenz Publications

ISBN 13: 978-93-93695-21-5

Published & Printed by
Noel Lorenz Publications
Noel Lorenz House of Fiction
Headquarters - Kolkata, West Bengal, India
154A, KCG Road, Kolkata - 700050
www.noellorenz.com

Peaceful Election in Kenya

Contents

Dedication

To both outgoing and oncoming leaders, youths, Kenyan partners, Kenyan sponsors, investors, friends, leadership aspirants and all the people who are connected with Kenya- a people of good will and lovers of peace.

You're the people who motivated us to spend our time crafting this peace preaching masterpiece so that we may preach, promote, encourage, inspire and teach peace. We all crave to live and continue living in peace.

And so, we dedicate this masterpiece for thy honour and honour of Kenya as whole. let's protect our women, aged, daughters, sons and lads. We preach peace.

About Book

We would remain a powerful country if we exercise peace in our country. One way of ensuring peace is through democratic process of election. We the ambassadors of peace present our hearty wishes to Kenya in this book. We mainly seek peaceful elections, healing from awful past elections, equality, equable leadership, peace campaigns and good utilization of national resources.

Writers are:

1. Samuel Nginyo(Kenya)

2.Eric Kyalo (Kenya)

3.Emmaculate Malii Nduku (Kenya)

4.Tamba J. Lebbie (Sierra Leone).

5.Amos Mkubwa (Kenya)

6.Ms Til Kumari Sharma (Nepal).

7.Thokozani Ndinisa (South Africa)

8. Mariam Oreoluwa Ariwoola (Nigeria)

9. A.L Maingi Ndungi (Kenya)

10.Ken Kagali (Kenya).

About Compiler ERIC KYALO

Eric Kyalo is undoubtedly Kenya's most prolific young writer and author assumed to be born in 2004, Eric went to Miu D.E.B. Primary School, Nturiri Boys High School, St. Martin Mixed Secondary School and B.C Writer's Academy in Uganda. His first work, Chronicles of a Poet 2021, launched him as a pioneer African Writer when he won African Literature Award. Since then, Eric has traversed the literary and motivational scenes with an array of works, novels, short stories, essays, poetry, anthologies, books and magazines. He is a seasoned and experienced writer and researcher who has published widely in journals. He has served as a consultant and judge in his writing career.

Acknowledgement

Noel Lorenz, we humbly thank you for thy support that you've showered on Destiny Ink Publishers, Destiny Ink Kenya and Destiny Ink Worldwide Writers Community.

The outgoing president of the Republic of Kenya, H.E Uhuru Muigai Kenyatta, we appreciate thy leadership. A leadership with a definition and example. We appreciate thy peace campaigns and development in education, infrastructure, agriculture and other sectors.

To Destiny Ink Peace Ambassadors this book won't be a success without thy contribution, dedication and unity. Let's keep preaching peace to the world.

Those whose names don't appear on this page, among them outgoing and oncoming leaders, sponsors, partners, friends and families whose contribution has been significant to us, we're humbled to quip that thy names can't fit in this page and thy names are indebly printed in our hearts.

Introduction

In 2007and 2017 post-election Violences we saw the face of death. We witnessed the ugly face of death snatching away innocent lives. People were maimed and murdered ruthlessly. People's voices and cries were never honoured by ruthless gangs.

Tribe rose against tribe. It was stones versus spears. It was bullets against bodies of men. Families were lost. Families lost their fathers, mothers, husbands, wives, children, other relatives and friends- their dreams, hope and breadwinners. Tribes were no longer brothers. Peace that always existed was destroyed.

Businesses and premises were destroyed. Some businesses died since then and they will never rise again. Nobody is willing to help such individuals come back to their financial situations. Nobody cares whether the victims live or die.

I can confidently say that the organisers of such incidents, who of course are our leaders, stay indoors watching televisions as young dreams are met by bullets. We're coming to such a point where citizens will know that they have always been used by these leaders. It's wrong to battle for a leader. Ye loose thy life yet their own lives are spared-it's stupidity. Let leaders enter into the field and fight themselves if they want fights. We don't want pretenders but true patriots.

We're colonizing ourselves. We're sending ourselves to the land of captivity where we were rescued by our fore fathers among them the late Mzee Jomo Kenyatta, Dedan kimathi, other diplomatic leaders and Maumau movement fighters. Destroying peace in our country isn't only disrespecting out peace icons but also rubbishing their tedious efforts into a pit. We should enjoy the struggle of the fore and founding fathers of this great nation.

Kenya is a theatre of valid dreams with an award winning talents. Why should we kill these talents without giving them an opportunity and time to blossom? These are the flowering plants of time to come. We need a peaceful country that is for all of us. Kenya is ours. Kenya is our country. Kenya is our neighbour. Kenya is our role model. Kenya is our icon. Kenya is our friend. We want to have peace in Kenya. We don't want propagandas, we want solutions.

To leaders; if defeated accept the defeat and wait the next time. There's always next time. So, why should you cause chaos when you get defeated? Are you normal or insane? You're not a Kenyan. In actual fact, you should be at our prestigious and treasured game parks. You can be a good tourist attraction site. In Kenya, we want real Kenyan leaders. A real people with both beauty and brains. Leaders you should be chairing peace meetings, rallies and crusades. We don't want flimflam of Kenyans. Take this; citizens are tired of thy cat and mouse runs. We know thy tricks. We want peace.

To citizens; time is here with us. Eliminate those 'goats' in offices just to enrich themselves. Sent them packing home. Elect leaders who carry thy future. A people ready to transport you to next beautiful Kenya. Take part in forming the government, don't be a part if observers. In addition, don't be lured by anybody to cause chaos. Tell them you love Kenya and you want peace. Don't be carried away by wonga and other false gifts. These are fake promises- lasts only for a time. Search a peace that lasts for an aeon. Better living in peace being poor all of us than enriching few individuals in a peace less country. Kenya is for us and we deserve peace.

To church leaders; Kenya is ours. Let's pray for peace. We're the custodians of peace in this country. God has placed ye in that position for a reason. Secondly, don't allow politics in churches. Let these people campaign outside the church institutions. Worship centres are centres of blessings. Politics can't be mixed with God.

And finally, to all of us, Kenyans, Africans, Asians, Europeans and all the human race, we deserve to protect Kenya, pray for peace and demonstrate it at all this time.

With one voice we say;

PEACE! PEACE! PEACE IN KENYA.

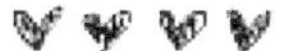

POEMS

MS. TIL KUMARI SHARMA (NEPAL)

She was born in Bhorle-Hile, Paiyun 7, Parbat, West Nepal. She is known as Pushpa in her surrounding.Her parents are Mr. Hari Prasad Bashyal Sharma (Mayor of village assembly in the time of kingdom) and Mrs. Lila Bashyal. She is youngest daughter of her parents. Her childhood was spent in her birth home, Hile-Bhorle. She had her school as Janata Ma.vi.Bhorle, I.A. from people's campus, paknajol, Ktm. She has her B.A from R.R campus, Ktm, B.Ed (English and population from T.U Kirtipur and M.A from Tribhuvan University (English department), Kirtipur Ktm. She has finished her L.L.B from Nepal Law Campus Ktm. She is currently doing PHD in English literature from Singhania University, Pacheri Bari, Jhunjhunu in the northern Indian state of Rajasthan (India). She is now in Kathmandu, Kirtipur, Capital City of Nepal. Her aim is to write about society, females, love, war, peace and world. She has published over 6000 poems, 180 essays and other few literary writings. She is a feminist writer. She is a professional writer in Nepal. Her aim is to change the world by her writings.

1) FREEDOM OF PEOPLE

The freedom to do right

Equal system to male and female

The democratic thought with in social justice

Equal rule for male- female

Freedom for moral justice

Employment and equal justification

No discrimination in race and outside of country

Education melts to humanity

The genuine democracy to equal Africa with other countries

The freedom not in vulgarity

But the moral culture

People in freedom to education, employment , gender and racial equality

2)POLITICAL LEADERSHIP.

Capable to make equal to world leaders

Securing the people and nation

The knowledgeable and skillful like philosopher

Not anger but with immense virtue

The loyalty and equality giver

The spoken energy with logic

Not money minded and greedy

Judge to all people

Not to move with money

Simplicity as people

Not snobbish and proudy

May be male or female in leadership

3)A PEACE LOVING LEADER.

Cool heart without anger

Cool and endurable

Keeping side the war

Guard of people

Equal to all

Shining with respect

Makes easy to people

Skillful to develop and artist of dynamic knowledge

Hater of war and love to feminity and existence

Democratic in moral right

Peaceful Election in Kenya

4) WASTING MONEY IN ELECTION.

For gathering to vote within battlement

Great waste of money

Poor people are dying in street

Who cares for that?

The money waste in poor cuts your sin

The filling hungry stomach of poor is the religion

No snobbish in winning election

Do good it as it is then.

Don't make vampire with waste of money

Do serve people with harmony

Peaceful Election in Kenya

5) TIPS TO LEAD.

Do equal to race, ethnicity and women

Don't supress women and race

Close the sex bar to secure women's body

Be humble to have purity of male / female

The right to marry and employment with individuality

Love the self-authority of people

Give moral Education

The light of feminine

Teach women to be powerful

SAMUEL NGINYO (KENYA)

He's a 27 years old civil engineering student at Endebess Technical Institute in Kitale. He was born in Eldoret and lives in Soy, Uasin Gishu County.

1) *PEACE.*

People of the great motherland,

Entangled to make it great and prosper,

And protect it from any danger,

Come and let's unite and,

End the hatred and tribalism in the motherland.

Peaceful Election in Kenya

2) WAVES.

They are with us now,

They shake all the corners of the fertile country,

As we welcome it,

Enjoying its breeze by clapping and saying wow,

But, are we sure it won't cause harm and make us cry?

People of the great country,

Why do we like unnecessary pollution?

Some things are not worthy for they bring no glory,

This is the time to think and take big caution.

As the breeze of the waves tries to cool us off,

Remember where you come from and your family,

For the waves are cunning and know when to pull off,

When they have sucked all their needs leaving you like,

A dried water lily.

Peaceful Election in Kenya

Great people of the fertile land,

This is the time to be united and live in peace,

Let us not root the evil by joining hands,

It is the time to be together and not in pieces.

3)WHY.

Why preach water and drink wine?

Why shed tears of a crocodile?

Why cook your words with delicious spices of lies?

Why point fingers on others yet you are the head?

Why are you blind to our suffering?

Why are you deaf to our cries?

Why don't you trust us as your own?

Why do you take us for a ride?

Why is it hard for you to speak the truth,

Why do you torture us?

Why do you leave us in cold?

Why? Why? Why?

Peaceful Election in Kenya

4) THE WITCHDOCTORS OF THE EAST.

They're well known for their deceit,

They walk all around saying they know how to cure,

They advertise themselves daily,

They say in their witches we should trust.

But I warn you play people,

Be careful of them,

They are just the same,

They will ask for small things,

Before they give you something.

They will feed you with poison,

Turn you against your friends and family,

Feed you with all sorts of wrongs,

When you're in trouble,

They're happily feasting.

Peaceful Election in Kenya

So, when you see them on the streets,

Ran away from them,

For they are like plague,

Just like a virus they will infect you,

Shut all the doors and windows,

To protect them from bringing their evil.

We all have beautiful dreams,

That one day as a youth,

One will sit down and listen to your words,

You will be leading people from north to south,

From east to west they will follow.

Peaceful Election in Kenya

5) WHEN.

We all have that beautiful dream,

That we will have a nice car and a mansion,

Wearing all clothes that are in fashion,

Having a nice white collar job.

But all dreams are shuttered,

Nobody cares of how you will be,

But seems as the youth as weapons,

Robots to be controlled,

For their own benefit,

They will tell as we are the leaders of tomorrow,

But their tomorrow never reaches.

When will they believe it's out time?

When will they believe we are talented?

When will they promote our own young creativity?

When will they fund a youth's business?

Without saying I scratch your back you scratch mine.

Peaceful Election in Kenya

ERIC KYALO (KENYA)

He's an experienced Kenyan writer whose writing connects both elegance and wit. With almost one decade in the English writing, his repertoire of experience has made this book the depth and scope it prides of, with an excellent trail of achievement to his credit.

1)TO ALL POLITICAL CANDIDATES.

When ya fail,

Know time heals,

Life is about facing the challenges,

And when ye get setbacks ye rise,

Dust thyself and move on,

More the wiser now and appreciative,

Life's many blessings,

Gifts and opportunities that ere seemed given.

And one day,

You'll get to that position ye yearn,

And ya serve human races as ye wanted,

But if ya can't accept defeat,

You're not a leader,

Your agenda wasn't about serving humanity,

You can still serve humanity,

While not in that leadership position,

Leadership is about serving,

Not power and position.

Peaceful Election in Kenya

2)2007 ELECTION.

The poll violence in 2007/08,

Led to loss of lives and destruction of property,

The scenario was repeated on a lower scale in 2017,

We writers and ambassadors of peace,

We hope it'll not happen again this year.

We have come from a situation where people were killed and maimed,

A number of Kenyans were displaced while others lost property,

And so for me and other peace ambassadors,

The country between these two is a positive gesture to this country.

There's need to remind ya leaders that there are internally displaced persons,

Who have been weeping to the government for ages,

And victims who were executed by the police especially the youth who were agitating for transition,

We lost a number of young lads while others remain with scars,

Though this is documented,

Peaceful Election in Kenya

Our leaders should ensure those victims who are still alive,

Or the families of those we lost, are given special recognition and solace.

Business enterprises were looted and destroyed,

Some never recovered,

And so, many people closed businesses rendering them jobless,

Our urge is that we shun violence,

IEBC should ensure all political parties sign a memorandum of understanding,

That they'll maintain peace during and after elections,

We all say; the ghost of political violence must be exorcised and buried forever.

Our country should not be on the map for the wrong reasons after every election,

This is why an anxiety is slowly creeping in,

Many people are afraid they may be confronted with chaos after the August election,

We don't want elections to take a toil on both lives and livelihoods,

We want fair and peaceful elections,

Peaceful Election in Kenya

The winner; is our leader,

No more fight,

No more hatred,

We preach peace.

Peaceful Election in Kenya

3)FROM THE DARK PAST.

2007/08 post-election threatened to tear the country apart,

But as most perpetrators went Scot free,

Survivors continue to live with the consequences of their altered lives every day,

We learned hard lessons,

That the violence was a stark reminder that the ogre of violence had not been slain.

Only the human rights activists tries to help us with counselling,

The things we were in a position to handle, we can't do them now,

We'd to curtail working in what we trained for,

We can't do menial jobs because we can't carry bulky things.

The last fifteen years our nation was in upheaval,

2005/06 were good years,

Things were going well but after 2007,

We've not gotten back to where we were,

We worry that if this happens again,

Peaceful Election in Kenya

We'll be in a big trouble,

We thought we would never stay in Kenya again,

We thought of moving to other countries as refugees,

These were very scary and unbelievable moments.

This is what we say;

We don't want these scary moments,

We want peace,

Peaceful elections,

One voice,

One Kenya.

Peaceful Election in Kenya

4)THE JOURNEY TO RECOVERY.

We've rebuilt,

Businesses have earned their wonga,

They continue to progress,

We're reaching a stage where we're recovering,

From the dark period of 2007,

The scars left in Kenya are beginning to shift to a more positive note.

Kenya hasn't fully recovered from 2007 and 2017 chaos,

Many lives were lost,

While many people who got scared fled;

A lot of businesses were closed,

Others like us have stayed,

We've decided to stick together.

Our people have come to learn that elections aren't the end of life,

This is what we're preaching,

Together let's devise ways to keep our young people busy,

Let's donate things to them for business startups,

Let's ensure youth don't only think about elections but their future.

Peaceful Election in Kenya

Let's peacefully support and campaign for our candidates,

And refuse to be used to create chaos again,

Let's have cohesion as the country heads to the elections,

Let's appreciate our efforts,

Given the fact that the country is coming from a dark past.

We bore the brunt of the 2007 violence,

But we've since invested heavenly to rebuild the business infrastructure that was affected,

Kenya looks beautiful and refreshing,

It's now the investment destination of choice.

However, there's need to worry especially if things go out of hand this year,

Then the future is absolutely nill,

I don't think anyone would want to live or invest in Kenya,

It will be challenging life if things go wrong this time,

That's why we seek peaceful elections.

Peaceful Election in Kenya

5)POLITICAL BATTLE.

The battle for August general election is taking shape,

With intense strategy meetings and alliance building, party affliction, community interests, proposed sharing of power and leaders' past development records,

Are expected to determine the outcome of the race.

Some leaders who lost to others are plotting comebacks,

Urging residents to give them a chance to finish the projects they had initiated,

As there is pressure from the voters who appreciate their leadership,

And what they did in previous terms,

However; voters have had an opportunity to compare them all,

Others will have an opportunity to complete what they had started while others won't.

Some have a vision in health, agriculture, education and infrastructure,

Others have special interests in talents,

We say all leaders are leaders,

Let political rivals hamper propagandas and clement each other,

Peaceful Election in Kenya

And be ready to work with everyone.

Political commentators have singled out party politics,

Development track record of individual candidates,

Ethnic alliance and choice of a running mates as factors that could determine winners,

But I say, those who have achieved a lot in previous ages,

Deserve another chance to finish the projects,

Other leaders don't know others played a critical role in their victory,

And we tell them to see eye to eye with their helpers,

We want peace.

Others are receiving blessings from elders,

They're picking tickets of the parties they trust,

But, people know what it takes to improve their lives,

They'll elect good leaders without bothering about the party they(leaders) will be running on,

The issue of ethnicity appears to be merging with pundits,

Arguing that whoever will pick deputy from major tribes could have an edge,

Peaceful Election in Kenya

But remember that smaller communities and others living in country can't be ignored,

It now means, top seat runners have an uphill task of scouting for running mates,

They should consult ere they embark on this journey,

They should listen to their followers,

Because we only crave for peace

Peaceful Election in Kenya

IMMACULATE MALII NDUKU(KENYA)

She's a second year student at South Eastern Kenya University pursuing B.Ed arts in English and literature.

1)WE NEED PEACE.

We need peace,

We condemn bloodshed,

As a nation we are tired,

The sufferings are enough,

Divisions we condemn,

The same language we speak,

One date should not be the case,

Remember for the long days,

You will need your brother,

Remember the eternity,

You will be with your sister,

Why allow one date blackmail you,

We campaign for peace,

Remember the long time,

You will need your neighbour,

This is a passing star,

Its light is unreliable,

Take care of all people,

Peaceful Election in Kenya

Tomorrow is unpromised,

We need peace.

2)A TRICK TO WIN HER.

Even by a laughter you can win her,

Even by a present you can tease her,

Threatening her makes her fear,

Why start a war against her?

It's much simple to be with her,

You just need your minds,

To think for an alternative plan,

To win her heart peacefully,

Compose lines arousing to her,

Show her how you plan for her future,

With creativity draw for her a map,

Of how her estate shall be,

With no doubt her heart shall be yours,

With no violence you will have won,

Where is it written a violence approach

Makes her open up for you?

Our leaders of integrity

You can win her heart peacefully,

Peaceful Election in Kenya

With no violence you can rule her empire,

You just need your minds.

Peaceful Election in Kenya

3) WE NEED PEACE.

We are tired of waiting for another war,

When it approaches these days,

It finds me like a surprise,

Seeds of the same mother cursing,

No recognition of the same womb,

Branches from the same stem,

Tearing each other apart,

May we please have the same voice.

We are all feeding from the same roots,

Sharing the same bark,

Sharing the same breath,

Same nutrients from our soil,

Will the wind bring about the division?

The wind shall pass,

The sane union shall remain,

Why give the wind powers to blackmail us?

Peaceful Election in Kenya

Our language is the same,

The difference is the tone,

Will the tone make us different children?

What we need is a structure,

To guide us to use our tones politely,

We shun the rising tone,

And advocate for the falling tone,

To balance us as the children of the same mother,

May we please lower our tones.

Peaceful Election in Kenya

4)THE SCARS OF WAR.

The marks of war,

Still fresh in our souls,

The smell of blood,

Still smelling from the soil,

The ugly scars we have,

From the last elections,

Could it be a pit,

For dumping innocent souls,

Could it be a pity way,

Of reducing our numbers?

When it comes to election date,

Masses are innocently slained,

For a win of bloodshed,

Can we please unite,

And apologize to our brothers,

And apologize to our sisters,

For taking away their blood,

For those Ugly scars,

Peaceful Election in Kenya

From our previous years,

Can we vote peacefully,

With respect to our siblings,

Can we care for our existence?

There is always life after election.

Peaceful Election in Kenya

5)MUST WE FIGHT?

Really must we fight a silly war?

To kill and die in such a bore?

Why kill your friend?

Why kill your neighbour?

Just because of a difference in an election opinion,

Do we really need to carry pangas and knives?

So as to win a name,

War is archaic,

Where will this violence take us?

Only pain, suffering and death,

Look up high to the colour of our flag,

White at the top and bottom,

White the colour of our peace,

The colour of radiance and pride,

Look up high and feel the freedom,

Look at the white colour,

And organize not for a war,

Let the colour guide you,

Peaceful Election in Kenya

To make a peaceful decision,

And run away from violence,

It is a shame to our leaders,

To forget our colours of peace,

And incite the natives,

To attack for votes,

My vote is a willing give,

Not a must give,

Let's vote in PEACE and not FIGHT,

No matter who wins the elections,

Let there be calm and greatness,

Let there be understanding and love,

But above all let there be democracy,

Justice be practised,

Let there be understanding and love,

Let there be acceptance and dignity,

Let's accept ourselves,

Peace is more precious than violence,

Life is a sacred gift from our creator,

Peaceful Election in Kenya

Why loose a sacred gift?

There is life after elections,

Let there be respect for life and existence,

Let our tomorrow be for the glory of our nation,

SAY NO TO WAR.

Peaceful Election in Kenya

THOKOZANI NDINISA (SOUTH AFRICA)

He was born in South Africa at Egiuwa hospital in Eastern Cape. He's a Xhosa speaking person who has written more than 10 books and 11800 professional creative literature quotes and teachings. He's the founder of E-Book writers platform which was established in March 1, 2022. Furthermore, he discovered the passion to do creative literature production when he was doing grade 5 and he was about 15 years at that time- during his primary school days. So, he has been writing creative literature for so long. He's a married man.

1) AWFUL PAST ELECTIONS EXPERIENCE.

The past is there...

So, we can learn from it,

Remember, there is no future without a past in this world,

Every single election experience must,

Teach citizens some certain lessons while it also makes,

Citizens to be aware of the empty promises that were made by the present government.

Awful past elections experience,

Makes citizens not to trust the previous government,

While sometimes opens doors for a new party to gain votes,

We can't deny political parties are different from each other,

And they have different manifestos,

They are pushing to fulfill once they are in power.

Past experiences should open the eyes of citizens to choose their government wisely,

Not only that but be able to make sure,

Peaceful Election in Kenya

They're governed by responsible political party,

Which is acceptable to its own citizens.

Let your vote change the past and make sure you choose a party which will work for you as citizens,

Awful past elections experience has made millions of political parties to loose votes from citizens who are hungry for change in their countries.

2)A CALL TO END POLITICAL WAR.

Why should you fight other political parties as a certain party which is looking for votes to govern in a country?

How long will you continue with these political wars we see among parties?

It's time of all political parties to end these wars we are witnessing each time in our world.

Politics are not made for parties to fight each other,

Neither are they made for people to start to hate each other,

It's time for all political parties to say goodbye to their wars they have for each other.

And the war they have created among their supporters and followers,

Everything starts now and this is an hour when peace and love,

Will rule all political parties and followers in all four corners of the world.

Let therefore every political supporter,

Rise up and stand for peace and unity,

It's time we see a different world whereby there is no more war among political parties and their followers.

Peaceful Election in Kenya

3)PEACE.

Where there is peace,

People will enjoy being themselves,

Peace makes people to enjoy the company of being around others.

Where there is no peace,

People suffer,

While sometimes will not have freedom to do anything they want to do in their lives.

Peace brings families and friends together,

Peace is an enemy of division,

Reconciliation and peace are the best friends you can find under the sun,

Reconciliation makes people to forgive each and make peace about their bad experiences.

We need peace every second in this world,

As we can't do anything without,

Having peace in our hearts in this world.

Peaceful Election in Kenya

4)PEACEFUL ELECTIONS KENYA.

Every citizen has a voice,

To vote for the party of your choice,

Show that you have freedom to choose who should lead your country.

Citizen should never be scared to decide which party,

They see suitable to lead them,

Let your vote be your voice,

And allow it to speak on your behalf as a Kenyan citizen.

My vote, my right,

My vote, my choice to whom I want to lead our country,

My vote has power to bring the change I would like to see in my country,

My vote will create a bright future for my children.

Go and cast your vote my fellow brothers and sisters in Kenya,

Remember you have power to choose who should lead your country,

Peaceful Election in Kenya

Let this election be peaceful and bring the need that will develop your country.

Peaceful Election in Kenya

5)QUALITIES OF A GOOD LEADER.

Leadership has the greatest choice,

Good leaders are seen by their fruits and qualities they produce,

A leader who has love for people will win many followers' hearts,

You can't lead people if you don't respect people,

Neither will you be able to lead people if you don't love them.

Good leaders are responsible,

Loving and caring at heart,

Leaders that have patience always succeed in leadership,

Yes, there is no development in this world if we don't have good leaders with good leadership skills,

Wise leaders have a listening ear and always improve how they lead their followers.

Wise leaders don't undermine people neither do they reject upcoming leaders,

A leader who can't groom someone to take over,

When he or she is no more in this world,

Has failed in leadership.

Peaceful Election in Kenya

Leadership is about caring for the people,

Being willing to nurse people's desires and wants,

Leadership is not for cowards,

But for the people who are bond and courageous to face anything that comes their way,

As a leader be kind and compassionate for people whom you are leading,

While you love all of your followers unconditionally and equal at all times.

MARIAM OREOLUWA ARIWOOLA (NIGERIA)

She is a poet, writer and student. She writes to inspire and change lives of people. She lives in Oyo state, Nigeria. She goes by the pen name Maryam Inks. She currently studies literature in English in the department of English at Obafemi Awolowo University, Ile Ife Osun State. She believes everything is possible except those ones we make impossible.

Peaceful Election in Kenya

1)PEACE WINS, VIOLENCE LOSES.

In its absence apathy steps in,

Causing small votes from the masses,

Without it, violence is resulted to,

Without it, birth rigged results.

Drenched in blood by not observing it,

Now who are to exercise their votes?

Of course it can't be liveless dead people,

Massacre are results without it.

Five years is not a joke people turn it to,

And a day speaks creates five years,

Ones of either pain, sorrow, ease, happiness or not,

Manifesto reading, propaganda are peaceful ways.

Election is not war but peace,

Either a lose or win game,

It should be given its own space to pace,

Peaceful Election in Kenya

This is the only ingredient in cooking a peaceful election,

Life of peace, gets, have everything good,

Violence brings gain, upliftment I must say,

And of course a peaceful election, births a peaceful reign,

Because without competition,

It's not called election but positioned.

Peaceful Election in Kenya

2)A CALL TO END POLITICAL WAR.

A CALL, A CHANGE.

War brings destruction, death to any given country,

Emigration now the only option,

Fears comes with voting, beef in government,

An unpopular government is later elected,

It aggravates, deteriorates rather than reduces and manageable.

Throughout the process of government,

Cooperation, unity discarded,

Birth rate reduces, death rate increases,

Suffering, maltreatment by unwanted candidate,

Family disabled and bribery by the aspirants.

When will thou end?

This is a wakeup call to masses,

And also to leaders,

Of course the led shouldn't fight,

Engage in war with themselves,

Peaceful Election in Kenya

Why not leave leaders to fight themselves?

Of course they would not,

So then, will there be nobody to engage in war,

Nobody to control, then they shall be back to normal,

Politics can be done without war,

I'm sure they will come to a realization.

Peaceful Election in Kenya

3) AWFUL PAST ELECTION EXPERIENCES.

A DISCOURAGEMENT

Bathing in blood,

Sacrificing souls,

Gruesome killing of innocent souls,

Threat of being killed,

Forced to vote and vote them.

Properties damaged,

Displeasing results,

Displaced body as a result,

Young complete family thrown into sadness,

Unheraring ears to people's cries.

Are those problems faced in past elections?

And they say once bitten, twice shy,

So peaceful stay at home is settled for,

As prayer is the weapon, the only key of a believer,

So hope the present will learn from the past's mistakes.

Peaceful Election in Kenya

4)*DEMOCRACY IN ELECTION.*

BY PEOPLE, NOT BY GOVERNMENT.

It's by form and not by force,

Choices produce fair result,

Money laundering enforced,

When traced sources should be found,

A government by the led not the leader.

With it the masses are in safe hands,

It's reliable than an archy dictatorship, won't be the order of the day,

There will be check and balances,

Only an undemocratic government is not checked.

So therefore, no bribery,

Say no to only spoken promises,

Why not elect promises put in action?

People see, do as for the leaders to see to.

Peaceful Election in Kenya

5)QUALITIES OF A GOOD LEADER.

A GOOD LEADER IS DETERMINED.

Laws punishable, should be punished,

Chance given to all in every activities,

Should lead by peace not by violence,

Should be corruption free,

Checking on people's welfare,

Development of the country,

Provision of employment for the unemployed.

Accountability matters a lot,

Should do away with hate speech,

Must have charisma, look presentable,

Of course must not have a bad past and present record,

And must not be a racist,

A country free of all these is sane,

Free from hard realities of life.

Peaceful Election in Kenya

TAMBA J. LEBBIE (SIERRA LEONE)

Was born on the 19th November, 2002 in Sandema village, Soa chiefdom, Kono district, Sierra Leone, West Africa. He started his primary school at UMC and later continued at SDA primary school, Kenema, Sierra Leone. He did his junior and senior secondary school at Government Senior secondary school Kenema. He started writing poems since 2019, and he grew love in poetry to express his emotions and feelings to the world. He's also a motivational speaker and writer who inspires the young to be enthusiasts of English. He became popular in sesquipedality because of his love for jaw breaking words. He's popularly known as the youngest sesquipedalian on the continent of Africa.

1)PEACEFUL ELECTION.

Election with peace,

Election with unity,

Election with transformation,

The hour has come for citizens to show their rights,

It is not a force and citizens should not be compelled to vote,

The hour is not to use guns to fight, but to use mind and knowledge to make transformation,

It is time to come as one to make peace because peace is unity,

THE PEACE OF LOVE,

THE PEACE OF DEMOCRACY,

THE PEACE OF TRANSFORMATION,

Citizens should not be abused or treated unjustly because they own their votes,

Youth should not be given drugs, alcohol or narcotics to fight and vote for the unwanted leaders,

Money should not make you forget the long suffering of the country,

POLITICIANS ARE MEAN,

POLITICIANS ARE TREACHEROUS,

POLITICIANS ARE NOT FRIENDS,

Peaceful Election in Kenya

POLITICIANS ARE TRICKY,

The use of violence can't bring a patriotic leader,

True leaders don't use force guns or violence to make transformation,

THE CRY IS TOO MUCH,

THE ABUSE IS TOO MUCH,

THE MISUSE IS TOO MUCH,

THE POVERTY IS TOO MUCH,

They campaign with social amenities which are things every leader must do when in power, but are they not used as a campaign strategy to beguile the citizens?

You should not be told to be wise to vote in an election because everyone will undergo the clap of poverty when the time comes,

VOTE WITH INTELLIGENCE,

VOTE WITH BRAIN,

VOTE WITH TRANSFORMATION,

Election is not a war and people should not be denied their rights to vote,

Election is not a disunity,

Is election not meant for citizens to vote for their own personal person?

A GOOD LEADER IS A BLESSING,

Peaceful Election in Kenya

A GOOD LEADER KNOWS THE WAY,

A GOOD LEADER SHOWS THE WAY,

A GOOD LEADER WILL NOT LET HIS COUNTRY DOWN,

ELECTION WITH PEACE,

ELECTION WITH UNITY,

ELECTION WITH TRANSFORMATION.

Peaceful Election in Kenya

A. L MAINGI NDUNGI

Born in Machakos, Kenya. A poet, short story, novel and guide writer.
Holder of B.A degree from Chuka University.

1) *SIUZI KURA YANGU.*

Yamenifika kooni, natokeza kuyamwaya,

Halaiki fahamuni, nafsi yangu kukoya,

Nipate yangu amani, mkishasikia haya,

Kura yangu siuzi, ujenipa milioni!

Nimechoka kuteseka, sababu kura kuuza,

Masaibu kunitwika, handakini kufukiza,

Kuniweka kwa mashaka, na dhiki kunipakaza,

Kura yangu siuzi, ujenipa milioni!

Visenti hivyo kunipa, na tele zako hadaa,

Ofisi kukuchupa, nayo heri kungojea,

Ninabaki kwa mapipa, maponeo kuyatwaa,

Kura yangu siuzi, ujenipa milioni!

Wapita kwa lako gari, ukivaa mamlaka,

Maendeleo sufuri, ukata kunifunika,

Kwa kufanya hiari, matatani kujiweka,

Peaceful Election in Kenya

Kura yangu siuzi, ujenipa milioni!

Kina mama sikubali, kupata hii miguso,
Vishilingi mia mbili, Nazi gora za maleso,
Baadaye kukabili, miaka tano mateso,
Kura yangu siuzi, ujenipa milioni!

Sikizeni na vijana, kunitia maanani,
Msije kupatikana, na kutiwa viganjani,
Walo wema kuwakana, kuteua maluuni,
Kura yangu siuzi, ujenipa milioni!

Wazee pia sitiwe, tamaa nayo makoti,
Kumpa uluwa mwewe, aso katu mikakati,
Mtapigwa na kiwewe, akishakata tiketi,
Kura yangu siuzi, ujenipa milioni!

Tunataka viongozi, wanasiasa wa hila,
Waulete ukombozi, na kutua ukabila,

Peaceful Election in Kenya

Wasitupe mazingazi, kutuhadaa kwa dola,

Kura yangu siuzi, ujenipa milioni!

Mkono juu kwaheri, ujumbe nimeshatua,

Wajue pasipo sisi, mabongo tumefungua,

Maovu hatusetiri, wala fisadi kutia,

Kura yangu siuzi, ujenipa milioni!

Peaceful Election in Kenya

2) *VIONGOZI.*

Siku tele kanikera, siwezi tena himili,

Yaniudhi hii Sera, hakika hats silali,

Si hofu Katy hasara, nalisema kulihali,

Viongozi wetu sasa, ulafi wenu kazidi.

Watia tele ahadi, mageuzi kuyaleta,

Walia mbeletu hadi, twawaona kutakata,

Wasoweza kufaidi, kisokuwa chao hata,

Viongozi wetu sasa, ulafi wenu kazidi.

Kura tukiwapigia, kidhani wana mafao,

Ofisini kufikia, inakuwa ndio mwao,

Ahadi zinafifia, watutema ja masuo,

Viongozi wetu sasa, ulafi wenu kazidi.

Tulotaraji suluhu, mawazoni zinabuki,

Mnakuwa kama wenu, nasi kuwa mashabiki,

Sipate Katy nafuhu, kila siku yawa siki,

Viongozi wetu sasa, ulafi wenu kazidi.

Tutacheka kifidhali, ofisi zenu muwapo,

Si' maboza kukejeli, bila kuwa na kitapo,

Msije katu tujali, mnakuwa enyi popo,

Viongozi wetu sasa, ulafi wenu kazidi.

Halo yenu yaboreka, kwa kuwa waheshimiwa,

Na sisi twazoroteka, kubaki kama wakiwa,

Haki zetu mnapoka, mkitaka kusifiwa,

Viongozi wetu sasa, ulafi wenu kazidi.

Sasa hivi naapiza, itafika yenu siku,

Nafasi kuipoteza, tufaao kuwapiku,

Mkome kujitangaza, tabia zake chiriku,

Viongozi wetu sasa, ulafi wenu kazidi.

Peaceful Election in Kenya

3)SIASA ZA CHUKI.

Jamani inaniuma, kusikia mambo haya,

Pembe zote kujituma, kidomo kuwayawaya,

Kuvuvia na kuuma, hatimaye mtamwaya,

Siasa hizi za chuki, ni wapi zatupeleka?

Kutema tele maneno, kupandisha ilhamu,

Kujitapa majivuno, Kuapa pia kwa damu,

Yatazua volkano, kuzusha mbaya filamu,

Siasa hizi za chuki, ni wapi zatupeleka?

Kutema tele matusi, na wengine kulaani,

Kiburi kama tausi, kujipeleka debeni,

Bure bilashi utesi, usoleta tumaini,

Siasa hizi za chuki, ni wapi zatupeleka?

Kueneza ukabila, dhuluma za wanawake,

Kutoa uongo sala, za mafamba ndani yake,

Kuzalisha zilizala, hofu nayo mtuweke,

Siasa hizi za chuki, ni wapi zatupeleka?

Peaceful Election in Kenya

Pabaya zatupeleka, kwenye zogo na zahama,

Amani kuwa mipaka, imani nayo kukoma,

Baadaye kuje waka, masihara kururuma,

Siasa hizi za chuki, ni wapi zatupeleka?

Mfahamu hatutaki, masuala mfanyayo,

Yataja zua mikiki, isofaa mambo hayo,

Urumo note kusaki, pia tele jakamoyo,

Siasa hizi za chuki, ni wapi zatupeleka?

Ujumbe huu pateni, amani yetu kutupa,

Sijitie uhaini, kututupa kwa mapipa,

Nanyi kubaki rahani, wenyewe tele kujipa,

Siasa hizi za chuki, ni wapi zatupeleka?

Peaceful Election in Kenya

4)AHADI ZA URONGO.

Ya mgambo napuliza, habari hizi kuleta,

Nawaomba kusikiza, wanasiasa kupata,

Taifa kupatiliza, mlio wa tarumbeta,

Ahadi zenu za urongo, tayari tumezoea.

Mnatupa kila Mara, burebure tumaini,

Maisha takuwa bora, kuwatia ofisini,

Kisha mwasahau Sera, mkifikia bungeni,

Ahadi zenu urongo, tayari tumezoea.

Msije hamu kutupa, ya maisha ya furaha,

Kisha kugeuka papa, mjitome kwa karaha,

Kutuacha ja mfupa, na maisha ya buraha,

Ahadi za urongo, tayari tumezoea.

Ni tele mliahidi, vipindi hapo awali,

Kusema tutafaidi, maziwa pia asali,

Mazuri mkayanadi, kutupa kusulisuli,

Ahadi zenu urongo, tayari tumezoea.

Peaceful Election in Kenya

Halafu mkapotea, tusiweze kuwaona,

Taabu zikatujaa, ikawa ndoto kufana,

Dhikini tukaselelea, pia vichwa kujikuna,

Ahadi za urongo, tayari tumezoea.

Mjue tunafahamu, ni mafamba mwatupiga,

Hanna katu hanjamu, ni bilashi kutuzuga,

Hatuamini dawamu, hata mkija turoga,

Ahadi zenu urongo, tayari tumezoea.

Nasihi wapiga kura, msije kuhadaika,

Na ahadi za kafara, zisoweza timizika,

Tutabaki kuparara, kila tukihadaika,

Ahadi za urongo, tayari tumezoea.

Sasa nafika tamati, habari kuwasilisha,

Nimeenda kwa kamati, wasije katu tutisha,

Kuiweka mikakatı, mkutano taitisha,

Ahadi za urongo, tayari tumezoea.

Peaceful Election in Kenya

AMOS MKUBWA (KENYA)

He is a poet, writer, co-author to WORDS TO MOON AND BACK anthology, script writer, rapper, content creator, human rights activist, ambassador to ILoveBlackPeople.com, CEO and founder of Black Art Eduintainment group Kenya, co- founder of Art Place Kenya. He lives in Ekerenyo city, Nyamira county.

1)POLITICAL LOVE.

MAGHEM IN THE MIND.

Oh God of all creation,

Bless this our land and nation,

Justice be our shield and defender,

May we dwell in unity, peace and liberty,

Plenty be found within our boarders.

Did you understand that line?

This triggers some quick tension and maghem in the mind,

Do they understand that and just do the corruption?

The grabbings, the drug dealings,

The cartelization of innocent poor citizen's minds?

But we still love you,

Yes, you politicians,

And this is my Valentine's message to you all.

Peaceful Election in Kenya

As citizens we tend to love you,

But your love for us lasts not long than a mere fortnight,

We dump our trust in you,

But you give your love to greed,

And what's painful is that you can't remember us until the next election,

But we still love you,

Yes you politicians,

And this is my Valentine's message to you all.

We need development,

We need to eradicate poverty,

We need jobs,

We need schools,

We need better health care,

We need stable security,

We need more and more water,

We need roads,

We need to boost agriculture,

AND,

Peaceful Election in Kenya

WE,

NEED,

TRUSTABLE LEADERS.

2)BLIND EYE AND MUTED.

Life is good but very hard,

Life can be hard but still good,

Am walking home from a busy hustle,

Just to come back fruitless.

Tired and exhausted I get knocked by a stone,

Thank God I didn't fall but fuck the shit,

This left me thinking whether to light a joint,

The only joint I had come with it,

Just as a take away.

Nope, I decide to stone the following morning,

Cause I don't stone past 7 p.m,

I keep my pace constant but faster,

I forget about the weed,

Thoughts of how the economy is pressing hard on us,

Leave myself meditating and wondering loudly,

Why should I vote surely,

Peaceful Election in Kenya

Lower food prices trending,

Their routine is lending,

And their role is feeding,

On the hungry citizens weeping,

They are the ones who do the dealings,

The poor citizens feel its feelings,

Worse is they assume and even fund most killings.

Before I make up my mind on whether to vote or not,

I find myself closing the gate,

So sad I had reached ahead of winding up my thoughts,

I assume everything like nothing was cooking in my mind,

When my ears meet head on with that unique but ordinary,

 Voice of my beautiful wife,

Welcoming me regardless of,

How hard life was turning to be,

Ahem! Thank God am home safely,

I pray silently as I receive a warm hug from her.

Peaceful Election in Kenya

KEN KAGALI (KENYA).

He's a native from Western Kenya, particularly Kakamega, Lugari, Mugunga village. He has a vast experience in literature and has participated in other publications of anthologies of poems such like "Pinaccio" and "Killing fate". A staunch lover of literature, currently teaching English and literature in Kisumu, Seme in Kombewa region, at Ridore Secondary School.

1.VOTER'S RIGHT.

I hold my ballot in my hand,

And say to myself there;

Is discourse to effect,

A real challenge to my future grand,

I have enough to expect.

I stay in a free country,

Where my predecessors were born;

Where tribulation rapture numerous times and sundry;

I feel the pity and the running forlorn.

Is not my fault to vote?

Another opportunity for election,

I'll teach young and old to wisely vote;

I bet no factions leads them in the wrong direction.

Independence of speculating solitaire,

Spicy spinning reels of sweet words,

Peaceful Election in Kenya

The patriots please vote wiser,

Elections build nations and kill corruption.

My version is to craft bedrock of just election,

And become a prudent citizen,

Liberty in the stared banners unfulfilled,

My rights at all to be deprived.

I'll cast my vote for the candidate I trust,

I bet for land expropriation I approve,

Wrong choices imposed as a must,

Time to tame malady of euphoria and move.

Let's rise! Unlike in the past!

And deny the chickened out democracy,

In it lies a catalyst for deceptive mistrust,

Endangerment to generations and noble country.

Peaceful Election in Kenya

Though someone dislikes time wasted,

Make the right choices to the polls,

This is our freedom so long awaited,

The right to vote is my right to freedom away from dolls.

Peaceful Election in Kenya

2.VOTE-BUYER.

When the ignorant voters sell their sick votes,

To the their ignorant exploitative vote buyers in politics,

Bargaining chip super rights of suffrage,

Then voters restrain the right to back,

And vote against buying politics and graft practices.

The vote- buyers once elected,

Nay, turns a blind eye on public,

Charging like whirlwind sprint of administrative quarantine,

Trying to control public opinion,

And quick fixing public offices in distrust,

Through political gimmicks and avarice.

The sick voter is a sick ballot!

Voting a sick bridesmaid is picketing chaos, imbalance and disorders,

When shall poor voters sit back against the malpractices?

Peaceful Election in Kenya

Poor baby voter is an aptly disgrace to election costs,

Poor voter faces cartel's angles of corruption and graft,

The braids grooming is simply extending the tentacles of power.

Peaceful Election in Kenya

3.AUGUST FEVER.

We are about to embrace heat and fever,

Of the coming elections this year,

Where political class will muster powers,

Pulling tackles to hunt down votes,

In the race of winning leader.

Some will be doing tricks and other options,

Some will master the art of deception,

Mutilating the voters' decision,

In the egocentrism out of notion,

Just to win the elective position.

Some will give huge penny over and over,

Or with t-shirts and 'lessos',

Inscriptions of their faces ready to tower,

This bewilderment should make thousands believe their power!

Some will promise couple goodies out of their slumber.

Peaceful Election in Kenya

Multiple of voters shall vote for such consideration,

Hopefully thinking is the best option,

Praying for sincere a rightful election,

As many had fashioned to vote in their own conviction,

Against the presidential election.

Majority speaks best wishes for choosing our leader,

Targeting local and national arena for own parameter,

Let nothing lead our house to another disaster,

Rather for greatness, protects for a year or over,

That would make a progressive nation ever after.

Let you pray and wish best of our nation,

Trusting our new leaders pure conviction,

That they may lead with no graft option,

Ridiculing corruption countering best solution,

For better great, development as a nation.

Peaceful Election in Kenya

CONCLUSION

A Destiny Ink Production

Machakos, Kenya.

I am convinced that you have enjoyed reading this book.

For inspiring messages, motivational talks, leadership training, poetry for: status, ceremonies, dedications and other events, kindly contact;

Destiny Ink production

Tel: +254731489614

Email: erickyalo517@gmail.com

~ THE END ~

~ ~ ~

WITH LOVE FROM ERIC KYALO

~ ~ ~

www.noellorenz.com

Peaceful Election in Kenya

Peaceful Election in Kenya

We would remain a powerful country if we exercise peace in our country. One way of ensuring peace is through democratic process of election. We the ambassadors of peace present our hearty wishes to Kenya in this book. We mainly seek peaceful elections, healing from awful past elections, equality, equable leadership, peace campaigns and good utilization of national resources.

Writers are:

1. Samuel Nginyo(Kenya)
2. Eric Kyalo (Kenya)
3. Emmaculate Malii Nduku (Kenya)
4. Tamba J. Lebbie (Sierra Leone).
5. Amos Mkubwa (Kenya)
6. Ms Til Kumari Sharma (Nepal).
7. Thakozani Ndinisa (South Africa)
8. Mariam Oreoluwa Ariwoola (Nigeria)
9. A.L Maingi Ndungi (Kenya)
10. Ken Kagali (Kenya).

Peaceful Election in Kenya